## How to apply your tattoo

1. Make sure your skin is clean and dry.
2. Cut out the tattoo you wish to apply.
3. Peel off the plastic top sheet.
4. Place the tattoo face down on your skin and press firmly.
5. Wet the back of the tattoo with a damp sponge or cloth.
6. Wait for 30 seconds.
7. Carefully slide off the backing paper.
8. Rinse with water and let dry.
9. Tattoo lasts for three to five days.

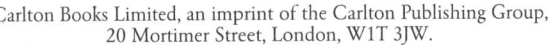

## Removal

To remove your tattoo, rub the tattoo gently with baby oil or use adhesive tape.

Carlton Books Limited, an imprint of the Carlton Publishing Group, 20 Mortimer Street, London, W1T 3JW.

J MAMJJASOND/11/6684 Printed in Dongguan, China.

Product function: removable temporary tattoos.
Tattoo ingredients: Acrylic Resin, Synthetic Iron Oxide pigment (Black)/CI 77499, FD&C Yellow No. 5 Aluminium Lake/CI 19140, FD&C Yellow No. 6 Aluminium Lake/CI 15985, FD&C Blue No. 1 Aluminium Lake/CI 42090, D&C Red No. 7 Aluminium Lake/CI 15850.

**Warning:** Not suitable for children under 36 months due to small parts. Choking hazard. Use by February 2012.

Do not apply on lips or around the eyes. If the product causes irritation, wash the skin immediately. If symptoms continue, seek medical advice.

Eczema-type reactions could potentially occur among users who have been previously sensitised to FD&C Yellow No. 5 Aluminium Lake/CI 19140

Conforms to ASTM F-963-08, ASTM D4236 and EN71 safety requirements.

CE

# THE PIRATE TATTOO BOOK

### Picture Credits

The publishers would like to thank the following sources for their kind permission to reproduce the pictures in this book.

Key to picture credits: t–top, b–bottom, l–left, r–right.

**Alamy Images:** /Nigel Cattlin: 15tr; The Bridgeman Art Library: /Daniel Maclise/Walker Art Gallery, National Museums Liverpool: 13tl /Peter Newark Pictures: 7l, 16l, 28, 29tr, 31tr, /Vancouver Maritime Museum: 15r; **Corbis:** 10r, /Lester V. Bergman: 1c, /Tria Giovan: 7b, /Lake County Museum: 13tr, /Lebrecht Music & Arts: 26c; **Dover Publications:** 6, 12l, 12b, 13b, 19b, 20, 21tl, 22c, 23b, 29bl; **DK Images:** 24bl; **Getty Images:** 24c, 25c, 27c, /Percy Robert Craft/ Bridgeman Art Library: 17b, /Richard Laird: 21br; **iStockphoto:** 3, 7b, 8l, 8b, 14tr, 14c, 14bl, 15c, 15br, 17t, 18t, 19t, 22b, 23tl, 25b, 26bl, 27bl, 30b, 30r, 31b, 32; **Jupiter Images:** /Brand X: 15tr; **Mary Evans Picture Library:** 10r, 13b; **Photos 12:** /Ann Ronan Picture Library: 4l, /Archives du 7e Art/DR: 5, /Hachedé: 16br, 18bl; **Rex Features:** / SNAP: 4b; **Thinkstockphoto.com:** 15tr, 23tr, 23r, /Brand X: 21bl; **Stock.XCHNG:** 1l. All other images: © Carlton Books.

Every effort has been made to acknowledge correctly and contact the source and/or copyright holder of each picture and Carlton Books Limited apologises for any unintentional errors or omissions which will be corrected in future editions of this book.

### This is a Carlton book

Text and artwork copyright
© 2011 Carlton Books Limited
Design copyright © 2011 Carlton Books Limited

Project Editor: *Paul Virr*
Written by: *Lara Maiklem*
Designers: *Joanne Mitchell and Ceri Woods*
Creative Director: *Clare Baggaley*
Production: *Claire Halligan*

Published in 2011 by Carlton Books Limited,
an imprint of the Carlton Publishing Group,
20 Mortimer Street, London, W1T 3JW.

2 4 6 8 10 9 7 5 3 1

All rights reserved. This book is sold subject to the condition that it may not be reproduced, stored in a retrieval system or transmitted in any form or by any means, electronic, mechanical, photocopying, recording or otherwise, without the publisher's prior consent.

A catalogue record for this book is available from the British Library.

ISBN: 978-1-84732-765-9

**Tattoo safety information:**

Carlton Books Limited, an imprint of the Carlton Publishing Group,
20 Mortimer Street, London, W1T 3JW.

J MAMJJASOND/11/6684 Printed in Dongguan, China.

Product function: removable temporary tattoos.
Tattoo ingredients: Acrylic Resin, Synthetic Iron Oxide pigment (Black)/CI 77499, FD&C Yellow No. 5 Aluminium Lake/CI 19140, FD&C Yellow No. 6 Aluminium Lake/CI 15985, FD&C Blue No. 1 Aluminium Lake/CI 42090, D&C Red No. 7 Aluminium Lake/CI 15850.

**Warning:** Not suitable for children under 36 months due to small parts. Choking hazard.
Use by February 2012.
Do not apply on lips or around the eyes. If the product causes irritation, wash the skin immediately. If symptoms continue, seek medical advice.

Eczema-type reactions could potentially occur among users who have been previously sensitised to FD&C Yellow No. 5 Aluminium Lake/CI 19140

Conforms to ASTM F-963-08, ASTM D4236 and EN71 safety requirements.

# THE PIRATE TATTOO BOOK

CARLTON KIDS

# Ahoy Shipmate!

There are lots of exciting stories about pirates. Most people have seen a film or read a book about them. But have you ever wondered what life was really like for those fearsome and wicked men and women that roamed the seas as pirates?

## A Hard Life

Pirate life was brutal and usually short. They often stayed at sea for months at a time, living amidst the ship's rats and eating rotten meat and beetle-infested biscuits. These rowdy, savage thieves lived and died by the sword, stealing from others to satisfy their greed.

Like many pirates, Captain Hook had a hooked hand.

**Treasure Island** is one of the most famous pirate stories.

**Peter Pan** features evil Captain Hook and his pirate crew.

## Your Pirate Tattoos

This book comes with a sheet of pirate tattoos – so that you can get a real pirate look. See if you can find this scurvy crew on your tattoo sheet. Don't forget – wear your pirate tattoo with pride!

### Crazy Captain Cod

### Terrible Tiny Tim

### Sly Sailor Sam

### Big Bad Bob

To apply your tattoos, just follow the instructions on the back of the tattoo sheet.

## Pirates Forever

Pirates have been around for hundreds of years. Ever since ships first carried cargo, pirates have roamed the seas, ready to attack them! The Caribbean once swarmed with pirates and they still exist in some parts of the world today.

*Johnny Depp as pirate Captain Jack Sparrow in the movie, **Pirates of the Caribbean**.*

# Pirate Fashion

*P*irate clothes had to be practical for life at sea. Their trousers were short so that the bottoms didn't get wet. Some sailors went barefoot as shoes could be slippery on deck.

Pirates often wore hats or scarves.

Coat made of thick velvet and edged with real gold braid.

Colourful silk scarf tied around the waist.

Short trousers, called breeches.

Long sea boots helped to keep their feet dry in stormy weather.

## Captain's Clothes

Pirate captains dressed in rich, colourful clothes and gold jewellery that they stole from the ships they raided.

*An old hat for protection from the sun and rain.*

# Women Pirates

Women pirates were tough and scary. They often chose to dress in men's clothes, which people would have found shocking.

*A sturdy woollen jacket for keeping warm in cold weather.*

*Trousers made of thick canvas were tough and hard wearing.*

*A sword or cutlass hung from a sash, ready for use in battle.*

### Tricorn Hat

A three-cornered hat made of felt.

*Pirates carried long swords called cutlasses.*

# Ship Shape

*P*irate ships were fast and well-armed for chasing and attacking merchant ships. They could also sail close to the shore to launch raids on land. With a large crew, pirate ships could get very crowded, especially if they were laden with stolen treasure.

## Eye Spy

A telescope was very useful for spying land – and for spotting ships to attack or escape from! A good captain could recognize different types of ship from a great distance away. Pirates nicknamed the telescope the "bring 'em near".

*A glass lens made distant ships look bigger and easier to spot.*

# Ship Spotting

## Barque
This ship was small and fast, which made it perfect to sail between islands.

## Sloop
The most popular pirate ship, the sloop was very fast and seaworthy.

## Brigantine
One of the largest ships used by pirates, it was good for long journeys.

## Schooner
This American ship was often seen in the waters of the Caribbean.

## Caravel
Pirates were always on the look out for a cargo ship like this to raid.

## Square-Rigger
Some of the largest ships afloat, they could carry a lot of cargo.

## Frigate
This huge ship was used to police pirate-infested waters and to guard groups of merchant ships.

## Junk
The favourite ship of Asian pirates, this speedy vessel could carry 15 cannons.

### Ship's Wheel
Pirate ships were steered with a wooden wheel.

# The Jolly Roger

The sight of a ship flying a pirate flag would have struck terror into the hearts of all who saw it, warning them of the horrors to come. Once its flag was raised, a pirate ship would chase down its victim before attacking and looting it of precious cargo.

## The Jolly Roger

The Jolly Roger is the most infamous pirate flag. It is also known as the "skull and crossbones". Because pirates had such a terrifying reputation, some think that the name Jolly Roger came from the old-fashioned name people gave to the devil – "Old Roger".

*Pirate ships flew the Jolly Roger as a warning.*

# Flag Spotting

Not all pirates flew the Jolly Roger. Many captains had their own flags. Here is a selection of frightening flags that were flown by real pirates.

Christopher Moody

Henry Avery

John Quelch

Thomas Tew

Bartholomew Roberts (Black Bart)

Stede Bonnet

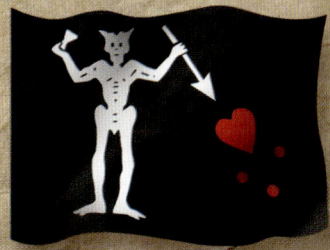
Edward Teach (Blackbeard)

Edward Low

Christopher Condent

Calico Jack's Flag

Calico Jack was a feared pirate of the Caribbean.

11

# Motley Crew

The number of men on a pirate ship depended on its size. A large ship may have had a crew of 300, while smaller ships only had about 20 men on board. There were lots of different jobs involved in keeping the ship running smoothly.

## The Captain

Pirate captains were fearless and cunning. They were in charge of the ship and led the crew on raids and attacks. The captain was also responsible for disciplining the men and sharing out the stolen treasure.

Pirate's Hook

A hook could replace a missing hand!

## Sailor

Ordinary sailors were rough and tough. They hoisted the sails and kept watch for other ships. They were also fierce fighters and always ready for the order to attack.

## Powder Monkey

Boys joined pirate ships when they were very young. They often worked as powder monkeys – a dangerous job that included loading the guns in battle.

## Blown Away!

Pirates could be horribly injured in battle. Sometimes an arm or leg would have to be cut off by the ship's surgeon. Hands were often replaced by metal hooks and legs by wooden peg-legs.

*A pirate captain had to be tough to control his cut-throat crew.*

# Life at Sea

Life on board a pirate ship was hard and dangerous. The food was awful and there was little fresh water. The captain had his own cabin, but the rest of the crew slept below deck with the rats, in cramped and smelly conditions. Lots of pirates got sick on board and many died before they could reach land.

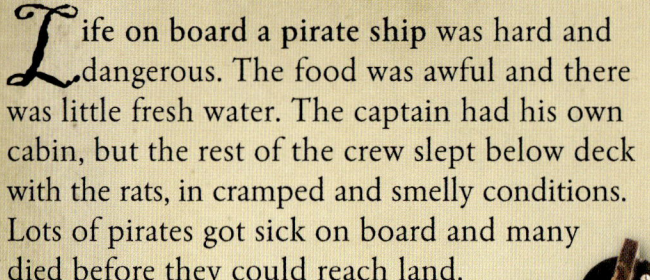

*Compass*

*Sextant*

## Navigation

The captain used special instruments to find his way, or navigate. A compass told him which direction they were travelling in, while a clever instrument called a sextant helped him to find his way using the stars, moon or sun. Pirates couldn't see a thing in thick fog, so they would keep quiet and listen out for the sound of approaching ships or land.

*Pirates listening in the fog.*

*Pirate ships were overrun with stowaway rats.*

## Scurvy

Pirates sailed for many months at a time and fresh fruit and vegetables soon ran out. With little vitamin C in their food, the men became ill and often died of a disease called scurvy.

*Weevil*

## Foul Food

Pirate ships carried food that would last and not go rotten. The meat was heavily salted and they took along dry biscuits called "hard tack". These biscuits were full of small beetles called weevils that you had to pick out or eat!

## Drunken Sailors

Pirates are famous for drinking rum, which they called "grog", but also liked beer and cider. Grog was issued as a daily ration while pirates were at sea and they drank it from metal mugs called tankards.

*Pirates would party whenever they could.*

### A Bottle of Rum

Rum was a pirate's favourite drink.

# Rough Justice

*P*irates punished each other as well as their prisoners. They had strict rules that were signed by the whole crew, including details of how treasure should be shared out. If any man dared to break these rules he could expect a terrible punishment!

## Walking the Plank

A famous pirate punishment was walking the plank. The prisoner was tied up with ropes and forced to walk off a wooden plank over the side of the boat. Once they were in the water they could not swim because of the ropes and quickly sank to a watery grave.

## Tough Luck

Pirates had to be brave. When the pirate Jean Bart saw his 14-year-old son hiding from the sound of the cannon, he had him tied to the mast during a battle to toughen him up.

### Message in a Bottle

A marooned pirate might send a message.

### Cat O'Nine Tails

The cat o'nine tails was a nasty whip made of nine leather thongs or straps. It was used to punish members of the crew who had committed a crime, such as stealing from another pirate.

### Marooned!

Being left on an island may not sound too terrible, but being marooned was one of the most feared punishments. It almost always ended in a slow, horrible end as the victims starved to death.

*Marooned sailors couldn't live for long without food or water.*

# Attack!

Pirates roamed the high seas looking for rich merchant ships to attack. Their fast ships could quickly catch up with the heavier cargo ships. As soon as the pirates were close enough they swarmed aboard, captured the helpless crew and helped themselves to the precious cargo.

*Pistols were popular pirate weapons.*

## Pirate Pistols

Pirates carried their pistols in silk sashes or large leather belts around their waists. Once the pistol had been fired, it had to be carefully reloaded with gunpowder and shot. The time this took could be dangerous for a pirate in the middle of a battle.

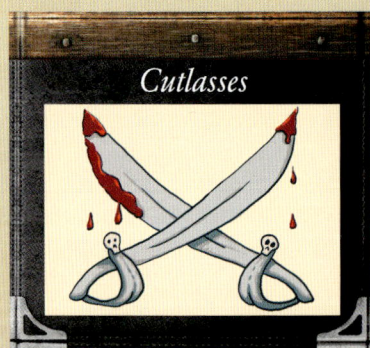

### Cutlasses

Pirates had to be handy with a cutlass.

# Boom!

Pirate ships had rows of cannon lined up along the sides. They waited until their ship was right alongside the ship they were attacking before firing. This caused as much damage as possible with the huge cannon balls smashing through the timbers and shredding sails.

Cannonball

Pirates boarded ships with their cutlasses and pistols at the ready.

# Treasure

$P$irates lived for treasure and stole it wherever the could. Sometimes they raided towns along the coast, but mainly they attacked rich merchant ships at sea. The ships they raided often carried huge cargos of gold, silk, spices and jewels. Pirates could become very rich indeed.

*Doubloon*
Pirates loved gold doubloon coins.

## Sharing the Loot

Pirates were very strict about dividing up their booty. Each man got one share, while the captain got two shares. Fights often broke out and these sometimes ended in mutiny, with the men killing their captain and taking the treasure for themselves.

*A sailor being forced to bury the captain's treasure.*

# Buried Treasure

Some pirates had so much gold that it is said they buried their treasure to keep it safe. If a pirate was killed without revealing the location of his hidden loot then it was probably never found. Even to this day treasure hunters are still searching for buried pirate loot.

*Who knows how much pirate treasure still lies buried in forgotten places?*

# Land Ahoy!

Pirates only came ashore when they had to, either to mend their ships or to stock up on fresh supplies. After months of hardship and danger at sea, they would make the most of being back on dry land. They would spend their stolen loot on eating, drinking and enjoying themselves.

### Crow's Nest

Pirates kept lookout from the lofty crow's nest!

Pirates often terrorized and robbed the people in the ports they visited.

## Shore Leave

One of the most horrible things about being at sea was the food. To make up for the rotten meat and foul water they had to live on while aboard ship, pirates would eat and drink their fill when ashore.

# Gambling Away

Gambling was banned on most ships because it could cause fights among the sailors, but the busy ports that they visited were full of taverns (places to drink) and gambling dens. A pirate could arrive with plenty of gold, only to lose it all playing dice and cards!

*Old playing cards look very different to modern ones.*

*Pirates spent their time ashore partying and gambling away their money.*

# WANTED - HENRY MORGAN

*Henry Morgan was a bloodthirsty pirate.*

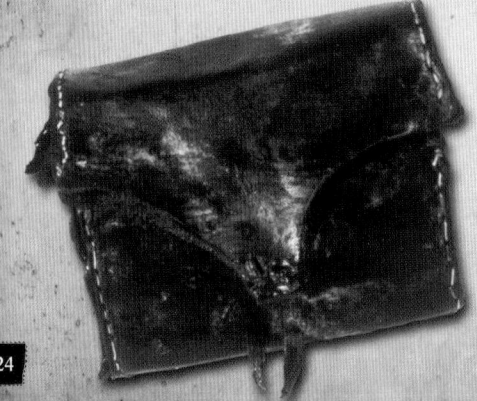

## Leather Lunch

Henry Morgan was a cruel and clever man who became very rich plundering ships and cities in the Caribbean. He was known for his savage raids and for killing innocent people. He once led 2,000 men to attack a city by land. Along the way, his men got so hungry that they were forced to eat their own leather bags!

# WANTED – ANNE BONNY

*Anne Bonny showed no mercy to her victims.*

### Dangerous Woman

Anne Bonny was a famous woman pirate. Dressed in men's clothes, she fought fiercely alongside her crew, swinging a large axe and showing no mercy to her victims. Swearing and fighting like a man, it is said that nobody realized she was a woman until she was caught and imprisoned.

# WANTED - BLACK BART

*Black Bart was a gentleman pirate.*

### Pirate's Tea Party

Bartholomew Roberts, also known as Black Bart, captured 400 ships in three-and-a-half years. He was bold and daring, but also an unusual pirate. Black Bart dressed like a gentleman and had very good manners. He never got drunk or swore and enjoyed drinking tea.

# WANTED - CAPTAIN KIDD

Captain Kidd was finally caught and hanged.

### Terrible Temper

Captain William Kidd was ruthless and bloodthirsty. He became so angry when his men tried to mutiny that he smashed a bucket over one of them, killing him instantly. It is said that Kidd buried a huge amount of treasure in a place called Gardiners Island. Some treasure hunters still search for it today.

# Blackbeard

**B**lackbeard **was one** of the most feared pirates of all time. His real name was Edward Teach and he prowled the Caribbean seas. He was a huge man with long dark hair and a jet black beard. Just the sight of him was enough to strike terror into his enemies.

*Blackbeard tied burning fuses into his hair to look even more terrifying!*

## A Big Softy?

Although Blackbeard was a savage and evil man, it seems that he fell in love very easily. It is said that he had around 14 wives. He got married on board his ship in front of his crew, who must have got very bored of watching their captain say "I do" over and over again.

# A Fight to the Death

Blackbeard was finally caught by a naval officer called Robert Maynard. They fought a fierce duel and Blackbeard broke Maynard's sword. A sailor quickly jumped on Blackbeard from behind and cut his throat. Maynard then finished him off with his pistol.

Blackbeard tied his beard up with ribbons.

Blackbeard's severed head.

# Dead Head

Blackbeard seemed almost impossible to kill. It took five bullet wounds and 20 sword cuts to finish him off! To prove to everyone that Blackbeard was really dead, Maynard cut off his head and hung it from the front of his ship.

# A Nasty End

**Pirates terrorized** the oceans of the world, but they didn't always get away with it. Navy ships patrolled places where pirates were known to lurk. Fierce battles would break out and sometimes pirates would be captured and brought to justice.

*Many pirates were hanged.*

## Death Sentence

Anyone found guilty of piracy was sentenced to death. Many pirates were hanged and some had their heads cut off. In those days people thought public executions were entertaining. They would turn out to watch and cheer, in the same way that we watch football matches today!

*A crowd gathers to watch a pirate have his head cut off.*

A ball and chain stopped prisoners running off.

# Pirates Beware

Dead pirates were sometimes put into a special iron cage called a gibbet. This was then hung up in public for up to two years while the body inside rotted. This nasty sight was meant to warn others about what might happen to them if they dared to become pirates.

# Locked Up

Captured pirates spent a long time chained up in dark, damp dungeons, waiting to be sentenced. These terrible, filthy places were full of rats and many pirates died of disease before they could be sentenced to death!

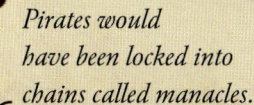

*Pirates would have been locked into chains called manacles.*

# Talk the Talk

Ahoy! – *Hello!*

Avast! – *Hey!*

Barker – *Pistol*

Belay! – *Stop that!*

Bilge – *Foolish talk*

Booty – *Any form of loot*

Brethren of the Coast – *The fancy name that pirates used to describe themselves*

Buccaneer – *Another name for Caribbean pirates*

Cackle fruit – *Chicken eggs*

Cat o'nine tails or "cat" – *A leather whip with nine lashes, used to flog prisoners*

Corsair – *Another name for a pirate*

Damn yer eyes – *A popular insult used by pirates*

Dance the hempen jig – *To be hanged (ropes were usually made from hemp)*

Davy Jones' locker – *A place at the bottom of the sea reserved for drowned pirates*

Deadlights – *Eyes*

Dead men – *Empty rum bottles*

Dead man's chest – *A coffin*

Feed the fish – *To be thrown into the sea – dead or alive!*

Freebooter – *Another name for a pirate*

Grog – *The pirate name for rum, their favourite drink*

Gully – *A knife or dagger*

Handsomely – *Quickly*

Jack Ketch – *The hangman. To "dance with Jack Ketch" meant to be hanged.*

Jolly Roger – *The pirates' famous skull and crossbones flag*

Lights – *Lungs*

Oggin – *The sea*

On the account – *The pirate way of life*

Rope's end – *Another word for flogging*

Sea dog – *An experienced old seaman*

Sea rat – *Another name for a pirate*

Sea rover – *Another name for a pirate*

Shiver me timbers! – *Said by pirates when they are surprised*

Splice the mainbrace – *To take a drink (usually rum)*

Swab – *An ordinary seaman. Their job was to swab, or wash, the decks*

Swallow the anchor – *To retire from the life of the sea*

Sweet trade – *Another name for piracy*

Walk the plank – *The short walk to Davy Jones' Locker!*

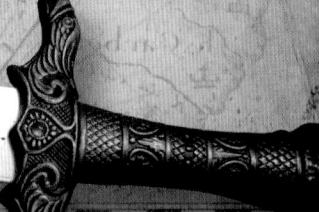

32

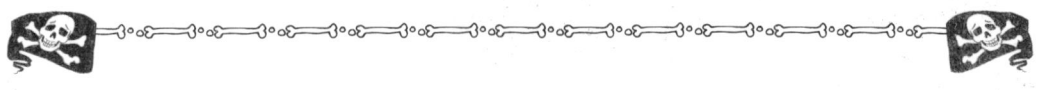

## How to apply your tattoo

1. Make sure your skin is clean and dry.
2. Cut out the tattoo you wish to apply.
3. Peel off the plastic top sheet.
4. Place the tattoo face down on your skin and press firmly.
5. Wet the back of the tattoo with a damp sponge or cloth.
6. Wait for 30 seconds.
7. Carefully slide off the backing paper.
8. Rinse with water and let dry.
9. Tattoo lasts for three to five days.

## Removal

To remove your tattoo, rub the tattoo gently with baby oil or use adhesive tape.

Carlton Books Limited, an imprint of the Carlton Publishing Group,
20 Mortimer Street, London, W1T 3JW.

J MAMJJASOND/11/6684 Printed in Dongguan, China.

Product function: removable temporary tattoos.
Tattoo ingredients: Acrylic Resin, Synthetic Iron Oxide pigment (Black)/CI 77499, FD&C Yellow No. 5 Aluminium Lake/CI 19140, FD&C Yellow No. 6 Aluminium Lake/CI 15985, FD&C Blue No. 1 Aluminium Lake/CI 42090, D&C Red No. 7 Aluminium Lake/CI 15850.

**Warning:** Not suitable for children under 36 months due to small parts. Choking hazard. Use by February 2012.

Do not apply on lips or around the eyes. If the product causes irritation, wash the skin immediately. If symptoms continue, seek medical advice.

Eczema-type reactions could potentially occur among users who have been previously sensitised to FD&C Yellow No. 5 Aluminium Lake/CI 19140

Conforms to ASTM F-963-08, ASTM D4236 and EN71 safety requirements.

CE

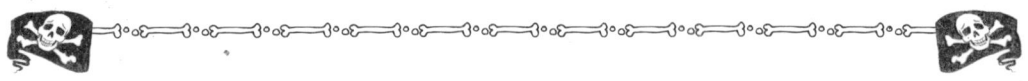